How I Made Money Using the Nicolas Darvas System, Which Made Him $2,000,000 in the Stock Market

Steve Burns

This book is dedicated to my stock trading mentor,
Nicolas Darvas. Although I never met him,
he has taught me more about stock trading and investing
than anyone else. I hope this book does justice
to his investing principles and memory.

CONTENTS

On the afternoon of January 4, 2008, the Dow Jones Industrial Average fell to 12,800. From the price action of the market I decided to take all my investments out of stocks and put them into cash. I had been selling out of the market during downtrends in late 2007 but something was different about this action. Money was flowing out of the stock market at a faster and faster pace.

The decision to move from equities into cash enabled me to keep my profits from the 2003-2007 bull market, which had grown my accounts to $250,000. I was able to keep my profits through the market collapse that ensued in 2008 and 2009. This book contains the lessons I learned from the books of legendary investor Nicolas Darvas, which enabled me to accomplish this feat. Hopefully they will help you through the turbulent times that no doubt lie ahead.

Introduction

I wrote this book to explain how Nicolas Darvas made $2,000,000 in the stock market. His books do a great job telling his story, but he does not use the same vocabulary as the modern stock trader and investor.

Darvas invested in stocks which had the best relative strength in the stock market. He practiced risk management through his stop losses. He was a growth investor. He did not know it, but he was a trend trader before the use of the word entered the trading world's vocabulary. Nicolas Darvas was able to control his emotions by avoiding live trading altogether; he put in his buy stops and trailing stop losses when the market was closed. By trading after hours he avoided the adrenaline rush of making decisions while the ticker tape was running and while live quotes were available. The ability to control your fear and greed while investing is one of the most difficult things to do.

He was a system trader following predetermined buy and sale signals. The system he used to trade made it possible for him to remove his ego from trading and simply work his system. As a trader, you must distance yourself from the wild emotional swings that characterize some traders, who need to be right for the sake of their egos. Instead, you must adopt the mindset that it is simply your system that did not work and that you will work on your system or trading rules after the market closes for better performance the next day.

The Darvas method is very similar to Richard Dennis' legendary "Turtle" traders of the 1980s. Some of the most successful traders in the turtle program became millionaires. Many of the top turtle traders manage millions of dollars successfully to this day. Like Darvas, they bought at new highs and went short at new lows which were made during specific, predetermined time periods. (However, they traded commodities not stocks).

If Nicholas Darvas had been alive in the late 20th century, I have no doubt he would have made millions in the Internet bubble by investing in Yahoo, Amazon, Microsoft, and other high flyers.

I also have no doubt he would have been in all cash by March 2000 with millions in the bank, unable to find any stocks making new highs. I also know he would have been in Apple, Google, and Research in Motion in the early bull market of the 20th century as these stocks doubled, tripled, and went up five to ten times their original prices.

While I write this in June of 2010, the stock market is at a crossroads. The Dow is hovering around 10,000 and the market is growing volatile again. I would like to see this book in the hands of investors and traders who are preparing to become millionaires during the next bull market, which will sneak up on everyone. You will likely get a glimpse of the next monster stocks as I did in 2004, seeing an early Blackberry and hearing about iPods. At that time I was unable to identify these products as the creations of explosively fast-growing companies. I had not read Nicolas Darvas' books at that time. I would like my readers to be able to check the company stocks of products and be able to determine if they are good stocks for investment purposes.

Are they at all-time highs? Do they have high expectations for earnings and sales growth? When should you buy them? When should you sell the stock once you buy it? How long should you hold the stock? I hope you will be able to walk away from this book with answers to these questions.

The next Darvas stocks could be alternative energy companies, hi-tech batteries for electric cars, some kind of wireless Internet technology, a company that revolutionizes the use of the Internet, or even something we cannot imagine at this point in time.

These stocks do not hide; they are found in financial papers under Stocks at 52-Week Highs; they are found in Investor's Business Daily Top 100 Stocks. The best way to locate them is to do as Mr. Darvas did: search for stocks at all-time highs that continue to advance on higher volume. With the age of the Internet and Yahoo Finance, this is a simple task.

It is my deepest wish that you are highly successful and become a millionaire during the next big bull market. As long as the capitalist system of the United States is in place, rest assured that millions of entrepreneurs and employees in corporations are working diligently right now to create a 'world changer,' as they have done throughout our history. It is like participating in a lottery that is won through ingenuity and hard work. When companies change the world, you can participate by buying their stock. This is basically what Nicolas Darvas did and how he made $2,000,000.

Chapter 1: Who was Nicolas Darvas?

In the late 1950s, a man named Nicolas Darvas made well over $2,000,000 in eighteen months buying and selling stocks. Was Nicolas Darvas a famous Wall Street trader? No. Did he make his fortune as a floor trader in the middle of the action each day? No... Then surely he was a full-time trader or investor focusing his every day, all day, on making his fortune in the market? No; he was a dancer, and most of the time he slept while the market was open.

Nicolas Darvas was born in 1920 in Hungary. He studied economics at the University of Budapest. He came to the United States in 1951 and was a professional dancer with his partner, Julia. His journey into the markets began in 1952 when he was offered to be paid in stock for a performance at a dance club in Toronto. He was unable to make the engagement but purchased the stock as a gesture of good will anyway. What he ended up with was 6000 shares of a small Canadian mining stock named Brilund at a cost of 50 cents a share. He went on about his business and a few months later he happened to look up the quote for the stock, and to his amazement it was quoted at $1.90 a share! He had made $8,400 in profit in only a few months by doing nothing but buying and holding a stock. Hooked on this fast money, Darvas spent the next six years obsessively trying to figure out how he was so successful with Brilund and how he could repeat this success.

Unfortunately, Darvas did not know that Canadian mining stocks just happened to be hot at that particular time and the timing was great on the purchase. When he began investing he had no idea where to start or what to do. At first he tried to trade different Canadian penny stocks like Brilund, but met with little success. He made the mistake of cutting his profits short, which racked up high brokerage fees with commissions. However, he always did a decent job cutting his losses when he felt a stock was not going to move up and make a profit. This principle allowed him to stay in the game as he was getting started.

I hope that readers learn this lesson from this book. Cut your losses short and move on to a better opportunity; do not be stubborn and allow a losing position to get away from you and ruin your account or confidence.

You can always buy the stock back if it turns around and begins to trend up again. This small principle of Darvas was a huge safety net that allowed his losses to be small.

Darvas the Rookie also made the mistake of listening to worthless tips, influencing him to buy stocks that went nowhere. Stock market geniuses are not hanging out at the local bar or nightclub, and they are usually not your coworkers at the office. The very fact that these people are offering tips shows that for the vast majority of the time, they know nothing. The world of stock investing is so complicated that the educated investor or trader does not offer tips because he would also have to explain proper stop losses, position size, the correct time to buy, and when to sell. If you do not receive all this information then you can be sure your tip is worthless.

Darvas next made the mistake of subscribing to worthless newsletters. The huge majority of stock-tip newsletters are useless. If newsletter writers could predict the future, they would be investing and trading and making millions, not printing a $2 newsletter and soliciting for subscribers.

Darvas put his money on the newsletter picks and began to fare even worse than with his random entries. He then decided to cancel his newsletters and get advice from a stock broker – one of those guys make a living in the market. This must be the key, he thought.

He was half right; stock brokers do make their living in the market by advising people which stocks to buy and sell, but they profit from commissions on those choices. They don't care about the direction of the stocks purchased; they care only that the account is active and generating commissions.

At this point in his journey, Darvas had read about 200 books on the stock market. His 'Bible' was Gerald Loeb's "The Battle for Investment Survival." Darvas stated he would reread this book about every two weeks.

The next stop on his journey was to become a stock fundamentalist. Darvas became wrapped up in the underlying value of a company versus its stock price through the P/E ratio, book value, and other measurements.

After extensive fundamental study, he chose to buy the stock Jones & Laughlin Steel. This was a steel company, and at that point in time all the stocks of companies in the steel industry were doing very well and going up in price – except for Jones and Laughlin, whose stock was not doing as well in price as the others in its industry group. Darvas figured that the stock was a great value for its price based on the value of the company.

This was one of the rare times Darvas was stubborn about an investment and did not cut his loss short. He just could not believe that this stock would keep falling in price. It did, and he lost about $9,000 through his fundamental approach. This investment failure really rattled him, and his confidence as an investor was shaken.

In the midst of his desperation, Darvas noticed in his stock searches a stock named Texas Gulf Producing that was going up. He knew nothing about this stock other than the fact that it was going up, and on a gut instinct he bought 1,000 shares and made about $5,000 in profits.

After this quick profit he became interested in the technical price action of stocks and how they actually moved, regardless of the fundamentals of the company underlying the stock.

He became a student of charts and price history. He learned that he should hold winning stocks but sell losing stocks quickly, and that there was a distinct difference between the stock of a company and the company itself.

Over a period of years Darvas began to understand that he must follow rules to limit his losses and not abandon his system when he became arrogant after many straight winning trades, and to keep persevering through his many losses.

He began to see the critical importance of timing in his buying decisions. He began to see how market participants pushed the prices of stock prices up merely on the anticipation of companies' earnings growth, far before the actual growth even occurred.

During his study of the technical price action of stocks, Darvas began to develop his techno-fundamentalist approach that would lead to his millions. After extensive failures, by which he learned what does not work, Darvas began to patiently watch for stocks that were on a dramatic rise on higher volume.

He began buying stocks the moment they broke out to higher prices. He bought a few hundred shares at first and then pyramided additional buys as the stock rose in price. He set trailing stops to lock in profits so that when the stock failed to continue to rise in price and dropped back, he automatically sold out and kept his profit.

These simple principles lead to Darvas' great success, accumulating millions in profits in 18 months in 1958 and 1959. He banked these profits before the market collapsed after his amazing run. He invested in Lorillard stock, the inventor of filter cigarettes (profit $21,052). He made a nice profit in Diner's Club (profit $10,328), which invented the credit card. He was able to lock in his profits in Diner's Club before American Express entered the credit-card business. He participated in the crazy run-up of the price of E. L. Bruce and had no idea why it was going up so fast. (There was an attempted takeover of the company via buying a majority of the company through stock on the open market) He walked away with $295,305 from this investment.

Darvas netted an amazing profit of $409,356 in Universal Controls stock. At the same time he made an unbelievable profit of $862,031 in Thiokol, the company that was selling rocket fuel while the space race heated up. These would be incredible profits for anyone today, but inflation-adjusted, they are even more amazing.

The fact that this was not a big trader at an investment bank working with millions, but a dancer that achieved these results in his own personal account, makes Darvas' successes some of the most profitable I have ever heard of from a risk-adjusted standpoint over an 18-month timeframe.

While Darvas did benefit from a raging bull market, he also had the advantage of investing during the right two years with the right system at the right time. The fact is, no one else reported personally walking away with that kind of money. So too, in the Internet bubble run-up of the late '90s and in the recent 2007 bull market finale, very few investors and traders walked away with the money they had earned in the good-time bull market party.

I wrote this book because I was able to take Darvas' lessons and do the same thing on a smaller scale. The Darvas system in its purest form can make you a millionaire in a bull market. His principles can make you an expert investor in a trending market. The Darvas system can give you the signal to go to cash before you give back your profits as an old bull market ends. You will also learn when to sell your stocks to avoid bear markets from ravaging your net worth. Let me explain.

Chapter 2: Understanding the Game

Whether you are an aggressive day trader or want to be a better investor, I believe this book contains valuable information and principles to help the aspiring stock market student be successful.

If you decide not to use the Darvas system in your investing or trading after you finish reading this book, you will still walk away with an understanding of how Nicolas Darvas and many other legends made fortunes in the markets.

If, however, you have the courage and persistence to trade the way Darvas and many others have, you realistically could end up a millionaire in a matter of years with a strong bull market to assist you.

How can I make such a bold statement?

I started with nothing and currently I am almost one-third of the way to a million. I have been using the Darvas methods in my 401K with great success for the past seven years, even though my options are limited inside the tax-deferred account. The system also kept my brokerage account in place during the recent market meltdown. But most importantly, I did not lose any money during the recent market meltdown, and that is the crucial difference when you take an oversized risk to make large capital gains.

If you give your profits back by letting losses run against you or try to bottom fish back in too early, you can lose sizeable amounts of money. That is why it is so important that you walk away from this book following trends while they last and cutting losses when you are wrong. This advice alone could be worth six figures.

The principles in this book are similar to the methods used to make millions by famous individuals such as Jesse Livermore, William O'Neal – publisher of Investor's Business Daily – and Richard Dennis of Turtle-trading fame.

At heart, all of these investors and traders were trend traders, making their fortunes by simply going with the herd. They got in at the right time when the trend established itself and got out when it was the beginning of the end of the trend.

They did not rely on predictions, guesses, or crystal balls. They were observers of human psychology through price action and volume. They rode the waves of fear and greed in the markets as they kept their heads clear and made decisions based on systems they had created, giving them signals on when to buy and sell based on probabilities. This gave them an edge in the market.

Just like the house in Las Vegas has an edge over customers and eventually wins through customers' losses, so to did the legendary trend traders make their money from the 80%-90% of traders who lose money in the market. While amateurs were selling when a stock hit a fresh high, the legends were buying, and sometimes the stock would go on to double. When new traders were buying a stock on a $10 pull back from a new high, the legends had already sold because they knew the trend was over by the volume and price action.

How did they know?

Nicolas Darvas knew through the price action and interest in the stock based on volume. In this book I will explain how you can do what Nicolas Darvas did.

What really causes stocks to go up? How are they linked to the underlying company? It took me many years to understand these concepts, and I will attempt to explain them to you in this chapter.

Where does a stock come from? When a company is privately owned, several investors may own a stake in it. When it goes public, an investment bank ensures that the company complies with all relevant rules and regulations and sells its shares in the open market.

The original owners will be allocated shares based on their private stake, but ownership is then divided into millions of shares for millions of partial owners. For example, if company A was thought to be worth $10 million, then the investment bank could create one million shares at $10 each and take the company public by getting it listed on one of the stock exchanges – the New York Stock Exchange, the American Stock Exchange, or the Nasdaq.

The money raised from the public offering would go to the original owners, and of course the bank would receive healthy fees for their part. The original owners could also decide to retain some shares themselves to maintain control of the company. Once a company is traded publicly, the new stockholders are all partial owners.

The company is then managed by a President/CEO who is accountable to the board of directors and shareholders for profitability. The amazing thing is that once these shares are sold on the open market, investors determine the prices. Stocks are not really tied to the fundamental value of the company, and the company's book value and earnings per share have very little to do with its stock price. What always determines a stock price is how much a seller is willing to sell it for and how much a buyer is willing to buy it for. That is the reality of the game. Investors' price bids for stock is the only true valuation. Perception of value creates the reality of price.

The major motivation for someone to buy a share of stock is the belief that they will be able to sell it to someone else for a higher price in the future. This is true whether it is master investor Warren Buffet buying millions of shares of a company to hold for ten years based on fundamental value, or an amateur day trader buying a few hundred shares that he hopes to sell a few minutes later for a $100 profit.

Once you understand the real psychology of the market you will begin to be profitable in both investing and trading. The real value of a stock is the price at which someone will buy it from you. There are times when a merger or buy out offer will bring out the true underlying value of a stock. This is when a tender offer is made to buy all outstanding shares of stock on order to purchase the underlying company. However, this is rare. Most stocks are bought and sold based on the psychology of the buyer and seller. Fear and greed rule the markets.

One buyer may buy into an uptrending stock for no other reason than greed as the price goes higher and higher. At the same time the seller might be selling from fear of giving back paper profits in the open trade.

Market participants vary. When we enter the markets we are trading along with hedge funds, mutual funds, large traders, amateurs, day traders, swing traders, long-term investors, pension funds, position traders, scalpers, floor traders, trend traders, endowments and sovereign wealth funds, to name a few. All of these participants have different reasons for timing their trades.

Make no mistake: the majority of market participants are professionals and do not enter the market lightly. There is no other venue where you can make such incredible profits through the click of a mouse. However, on the other hand, you can also lose a lot of money if you don't know what you are doing. You are dealing with professionals who generally take money away from the majority of amateurs.

When investing and trading, you must have a system that over time outperforms the market. I will show you in this book how Nicolas Darvas gave me the principles and system to prosper in the markets during the amazing bull run of the early 21st century, and more importantly, how to keep my profits from the meltdown that followed.

Nicolas Darvas was able to see the market for the game that it was. As you will learn in this book, legendary investor Nicolas Darvas controlled his emotions while creating a system for making money in the stock market based on other investors' fear and greed. The key was to follow a system and not make decisions based on opinions.

Darvas understood that future earnings expectations drove stock prices up, but he only bought particular stocks that were already being driven up by increased volume. He was a trend trader; he bought into stocks that were in uptrends and held them until the trend reversed strongly, then sold out and locked in his profits with automatic stop loss orders. He was a master of the game, and my goal is that when you finish reading this book you will have all the knowledge you need to use Darvas' system and principles to win the stock market game yourself.

Chapter 3: Thinking like Nicolas Darvas

How did a dancer turn a few thousand dollars into over $2 million in less than two years? How did a guy shun all of Wall Street's advice about investing and set out on his own to make a fortune doing what was contrary to common sense? Why buy when a stock is going to an all-time high? Sell quickly and take a loss when it falls, instead of waiting for it to go back up? Ignore all of the underlying business valuations of a stock with its P/E ratios, book values, and growth projections that are supposed to tell you if it is a good value for its price?

Surely this is not the path to a fortune. What is most shocking is that Darvas let his profits run and did not make profits until the stock fell dramatically. Yet as shocking as these methods appear, this is indeed how a dancer who invested in stocks in the '50s and early '60s made a fortune.

But what is most impressive is that Darvas kept his fortune and did not lose it in the nasty bear markets of the late '60s and early '70s. I have seen many people make money by investing, stock trading, or day trading, and then give it all back and then some. The latest bear market of 2008 and 2009 has shown this dramatically, even for buy-and-hold investors.

Who was this dancer who became a stock market wizard? His name was Nicolas Darvas, and he did what every budding stock investor and trader dreams of doing: He became a millionaire in a short amount of time.

My point in writing this book is to share with my readers that it is possible – that in both bull and bear markets it is possible to make an amazing sum of money. The most important thing is to use the principles outlined in this book when the next bull market comes around, as this is when the

Darvas methods work best. You can also use variations of his methods to trade stocks within boxes for profit.

In his third book Darvas also explained how to short stocks, even though the method did not fit his own personality. It fits my personality, however, and I have made nice profits shorting on several occasions.

In his books, Darvas taught the important lesson that it is OK to go to cash and to exit the stock market completely. This is a lesson I wish I had understood during the crash of 2000. I lost about $30,000 in my company profit-sharing plan when I kept trying to go back in as I anticipated a rebound in the glorious technology sector.

The devoted buy-and-holders among us watched their investment portfolios melt by 50% from late 2007 to March 2009. The Darvas method would have prompted you to get out as your investment dropped below the price of its established price box. The method would have even given you the signal to go short.

To think like the legendary investor Nicolas Darvas you must have an urge to buy a stock when it breaks to a new high and have no desire to bottom fish a falling stock or to try to get a great value for your money.

You want a stock that is in a growing industry and that people have ridiculous earnings expectations from. You don't care about the fundamental value of the underlying business – you care that everyone wants to buy the stock. You care that it has been going up for some time and just popped up to yet another new high. Your favorite time to buy a stock is when everyone that is holding it is sitting on a profit at an all-time high, and there is no one holding it with a loss waiting to break even.

You do not think about diversity; you simply pick one,

two, three, or maybe even four stocks that you like, let the winners run, and sell the ones that fail to continue to run.

Your opinion has little to do with your investing and trading. You let the winning horses run and put the losers out to pasture. You do not take profits prematurely, and the only reason you sell a stock is if it fails to stay in its topmost price range, or as Darvas called it, the stock's price box.

You keep your ego out of your investing. You trade according to a system. If you don't make money, you did not fail – your system failed. You are a success if you followed your system.

Failure is the result of not following your predetermined system. Losing money is not a failure if you followed your system. It is dangerous to not cut your losses when it is time. It is also a mistake if you did not enter an automatic buy stop to take a position when a stock on your watch list broke to a new high.

To think like Darvas, you have to make judgments on how much room to allow a stock to move based on its personality. Some stocks swing wildly in 10-point boxes and may need more room to fluctuate than others. Some stocks will be too volatile for your personality and some will be too boring to hold. Darvas' system suited his personality, and you may have to adjust his system to suit your personality. However his principles of discipline, the right mindset, system management, cutting losses short, letting profits run, always buying into strength while buying with the increasing volume, and going into cash at the right time are universal for all traders.

To think like Nicolas Darvas you must have the desire to buy high at the right time, believing that you will sell at a higher price later. You must allow the market to tell you what to do and stop trying to predict. Your desire must be to bet on the biggest and fastest horse that has won the most races.

Chapter 4: Entering the Game

There are many ways to get into the game on Wall Street. Like Nicolas Darvas himself, you can open a brokerage account and get approved to use margin. This will enable you to invest and trade with double the amount of cash you deposit.

In other words, you can deposit $10,000 in a brokerage account and then purchase $20,000 worth of stocks; with this leverage you can double your profits in an uptrend, but be warned – you can also double your losses in a downtrend.

You can also enter the game through a traditional 401K through your job. It's amazing to me that many people do not participate in 401Ks at work when their employer offers matching contributions.

If you want to build wealth, this is one of the greatest ways to do it. If your employer matches your contributions by 10% of your salary, then 10% of your salary will be deducted into your 401K each pay period.

If you earn $52,000 a year, you will contribute $5,200 annually to your 401K, which is $100 a week. Your $100 will be matched with your employer's $100, giving you $200 total into your account. Plus, if you are in a 15% income tax bracket, you will also save that $15 in taxes each week, allowing it to grow tax deferred until you retire.

You can also expand your account with the Darvas Box System by buying into the market only during uptrends and going back to cash in downtrends. You can invest your 401K money in the stock market through an S&P fund, stock mutual funds, or your company's stock if that is an option.

Yes, you may have been told by the mainstream media

or financial advisers that investing your retirement money in your company's stock is way too risky. The risks are there, but greatly exaggerated; if you trade following the Darvas method, the odds are in your favor and you should do very well.

If your company is making all-time highs, it is unlikely to end up like Enron, Global Crossing, General Motors, Lehman Brothers, or Bear Stearns. Even these company employees had a few days to get out of the stock when the rumors (and the reality) surfaced about them. Do not let these odd examples steer you away from investing with your own company; the key is to get out the moment the stock loses support in its box – that very moment, without hesitation.

But these are the worst-case examples. What about employees who worked for Apple, Google, Walmart, or Microsoft during their startup? These undiversified investors are now millionaires; they could have not been "risky" and work for 30 more years.

This is not some crazy, risky scheme; this is how Darvas invested, sometimes only holding two stocks in his portfolio but rarely more than four. Even legendary investor Warren Buffet claimed: "Diversity is for those that do not know what they are doing."

Do not, however, invest in your company stock if you are going to simply buy and hold it. The odds are against you, and eventually, over a long enough period of time, the stock will crash, as most stocks do eventually crash when companies fall out of favor with the markets.

If, however, you actively manage your account and follow the Darvas box method, you can make very outsized returns in bull markets, or a fortune if you are the one who works at an Apple, Google, or Walmart when the company is first growing at a rapid speed.

I grew my own 401K by more than 20% a year for several years straight as my company stock rocketed from $28 to $103 a share from 2003-2007.

I was limited to putting only 50% of my funds in my stock, which kept my total returns down significantly, but such a return is still world class. I also received options on my company stock from 2003-2007. I was able to exercise all of them at close to the peak each year, and the last options for $99 a share. But once again, I was able to remove my valuable 401K money from my company into a cash position before the meltdown started and it fell through its top price box. By 2009, the stock fell all the way back to $46 a share. I did not reenter my company stock until it safely broke a 52-week high in 2010 at $81.

At that time I bought 1000 shares; it raced to $85 in two days but my happiness soon turned into disappointment as I sold when it rapidly fell to $81. After I was out it fell under $80 and back into the $79 range. The Darvas method for buying into an uptrend does not work as well in a slow market. The money is made in the high-volume bull markets. However the fact that it keeps you out of the bear market is one of its main strengths.

Do yourself the biggest financial favor and open a 401K today if one is available to you. Put in enough money to get a full company match. Also, open a brokerage account. Start with whatever means you have wherever you are.

Most legendary traders began with little and grew their accounts over years of careful system following. Do not concern yourself with size at first. Nicolas Darvas started with a few thousand dollars that he turned into millions. If we do what he did we can get the same results. I know because I have, and I was richly rewarded. Take that first step. Do it for yourself and for your family.

Chapter 5: Learning from Losing

In the late 1990s I began receiving contributions into a profit-sharing plan from my company.

The contributions were between 7%-12% of my pay each year. Employees could put this money in the company's stock or mutual funds. I chose the most aggressive funds available to me at the time.

These funds were invested in technology companies and in Internet stocks. This was good timing as my paltry few thousand dollars a year in contributions grew to an amazing $60,000 by March of 2000. I was receiving account statements that showed 40% to 50% annual gains in funds as the NASDAQ made its amazing climb to 5000.

I was only 28 years old, and I figured I was a stock market genius: I would always take on as much risk as possible and be richly rewarded for it. While there are many genius investors, traders, hedge fund managers, and entrepreneurs during raging bull markets, most of these wizards are usually crushed by losses when their particular strategy stops working as the markets change, and they have no other system for making money. This is what happened to me, as I was calculating how my account would grow exponentially over the next few years as the Internet exploded and the profits rolled in.

The market was setting up for a top and collapse. I will never forget coming home from work and watching CNBC as they celebrated the NASDAQ breaking the 5000 barrier and discussed hopes for the future.

This was a red-flag day for a top. 5000 was that psychological breakthrough point into a new mega price box that would not hold. This is a lesson I understand now, after having experienced huge losses from 2000-2002. After I watched my account fall from $60,000 in March of 2000 to a paltry $29,000 at the depths of the bear market in the first quarter of 2003, I promised myself that I would never again give back my profits once I made the money back. If I had a second chance in a bull market to acquire another big account, I would keep it.

The main difficulty I have noted in trading and investing over the past fifteen years is not in the making of profits but in keeping those profits. You must know when to make oversized profits by buying into leading stocks when new annual highs are made in the market.

I completely disagree with buy-and-hold investing. The advice of buy and hold is simply long-term, 10-30 year trend trading wherein pundits believe that the long-term uptrend in the market will continue.

Whether it does or not, there are many simple ways to outperform the market. The most useful method is to simply go from stock mutual funds to cash equivalents when a nasty recession begins. To quantify this in technical terms, the best technique I have observed is simple moving averages. Sell and go to cash when the S&P 500 dips below its 200-day moving average. This is the best sign of a bear market. Do not buy back in until it crosses above a 200-day moving average. This one system doubles the return of stocks versus just buying and holding. The 200-day simple moving average is available on Yahoo! Finance.

Recession is expected because unemployment is climbing and the stock market is falling. The number one clue is when the market fails to make new highs. Staying in a market that is going down day after day is not a good way to make money in the market. Buying into a market as it is crashing is the perfect way to lose money and to lose sleep.

This was a lesson I learned only after reading Nicolas Darvas' books explaining price boxes. However this lesson yielded great payoffs in 2007-2008 as a downtrend began and I found fewer opportunities to invest and trade. This left me in cash as the stock market plunged and my capital was safely on the sidelines earning interest.

My 2000-2003 losses totaled well over $40,000, which was a huge sum of money for me. In those years I was a buy-and-hold investor, waiting for the rebound in the stock market. I did this out of ignorance rather than intelligence. I would have been much better off had I know about the Darvas methods back then or had I at least used the 200-day moving averages as buy-and-sell indicators.

I prepared myself to earn my money back and to keep it. I became interested when the strong rally in the market heated up in 2003 and I noticed my own company's stock jumping aggressively from a price in a $15/$19 box to suddenly breaking at $23. Little did I know that my company's stock, Delhaize Group, would rocket from the teens to over $103.90 a share by 2007. By that time, I traded it all way up through many boxes and escaped like a bandit with my profits!

Chapter 6: How to Manage Risk

Risk is the element in your trading that allows for profit. The main thing you do as trader is manage risk. Your number one rule is: Control your losses. Darvas did this so well with his stop losses. In setting predetermined stops before he entered a trade, Darvas measured his risk and controlled it upfront. His upside was hypothetically unlimited, but his downside was measured and controlled by studying and understanding the price history and action of the stock itself. Before Darvas purchased a stock he understood the price range that the stock was currently trading in. He looked at price history to determine the key resistance point where the stock had trouble moving higher, and at the supporting price where the stock stopped dropping and buyers moved in.

He used what he saw to set his stops. If a stock was in a price range of 50/55, then he would put in a buy stop at $55.01. (In Darvas' time period, stocks were traded in fractions so these are hypothetical examples in decimals). In most instances, if the price broke through and reached $58, Darvas would follow up with a stop loss at $54.99. If the stock was truly in an uptrend it would not fall back into an old price box, and it was expected to continue to move up and attract more buyers. The old resistance became the new support. This juncture is essentially a second opportunity for buyers who lost to buy on the breakout.

Darvas also managed risk by giving back his profits in a stock through trailing his stop loss up as the price rose. A major risk in trading is to not lock in profits when they are there. I have read horror stories of people who bought into Internet companies in the late '90s and held the stocks and become millionaires on paper, but never locked in their profits. These investors watched a few thousand dollars in stocks grow into over a million dollars; they also watched their profits dwindle into a few thousand dollars. This is truly heartbreaking, and I am sure very stressful.

You must follow Darvas' lead and set your stops to take profits out of the market when the market begins to move against you. As we have discussed, these trailing stops should follow the stock as it trends upwards and be at the top of an old box as the stock breaks to a new price box. If the stock returns to its previous high you can buy it back and join in the next leg of the rally. If it never returns to that high, you have locked in profits and avoided the terrible downtrends that engulf the hottest growth stocks as bear markets begin. Your main tools for managing risk are the stop loss and the trailing stop. Through these money management techniques you protect the risk of losing your original capital and avoid the risk of giving back your hard-earned profits.

It is surprising to learn that buying when a stock is at a high in hopes of selling it at an even higher price is much less risky than buying as it falls to a lower low with the hope that it will rise back to a previous high price.

Save your bargain-hunting for the grocery store. When stock trading and investing, buy the strongest stock in the strongest sector the moment it makes a new high out of an established box. This is how the most successful traders of all times traded.

The stock market is a democracy wherein each trade is a vote. When all participants are voting on a stock to go up, cast your vote alongside them by buying that stock. At that point the odds are in your favor as it unlikely that the stock will suddenly reverse. It is possible and it does happen, but controlling risk is about making high-probability winning trades, which lowers overall risk.

Buying into a declining stock as it makes lower lows is very risky. Everyone is casting their votes on a declining price. Going against the majority and buying a stock while it is declining is a good way to pay 'stupid' trader tax. A falling stock can accelerate in the plunge when fear takes over, and buying in at the first sign of strength is usually a fool's game called a "dead cat bounce." Always swim in the same direction as the river flows; to swim against the river is risky and dangerous.

When the market is increasing on heavy buying, go with the flow and lock in profits as it goes; trends work because when a stock makes a new high, it means that all traders and investors are sitting on a profit. Who sells a stock when they are winning? When greed kicks in, stockholders start imagining huge profits and hold on until they are spooked by a correction. On the other hand, when a stock is at all-time lows, every stockholder is sitting on a loss, hoping to get out at a better price; hence, the stock price has to climb a wall of worry. As each old price box is reached, stockholders think: "Thank goodness; now I can get out at the price at which I purchased this stock." The stock meets a tremendous amount of selling pressure the whole way back up. This is why it is so important to buy stocks at all-time highs and avoid all the pent-up selling when trying to regain an old high.

In Darvas' third book he advises never to lose more than 10% on a losing stock and never to give back more than 20% in profits on a wining stock. This is the most you should risk. However, most price boxes are less than 10%, and the tops of previous boxes for winners are usually far less than 20%. I would advise using these percentages as hard stops. If the stock you are watching has price boxes greater than 10%, then the stock is probably too volatile to invest in. It may also stop you out because of wild swings in price, or you may not have the stomach for a particular stock's personality.

Some stocks behave like crazy spouses, initially pampering you and giving you gifts; then they suddenly act crazily and take everything back. Invest in stocks that fit your personality and your risk tolerance. Darvas stocks stay in a steady uptrend and inside their price boxes until the breakout, after which they leave their boxes and do not return until they stop trending. Darvas also recommends only watching three or four winning stocks at a time so as not to dilute your attention among many stocks. Price boxes should be established over at least three weeks. Buy at the moment of a breakout; do not chase a stock that has already run through a box in a few days and is making new highs for a second time. In those instances, you are usually buying the top of a new price box where it will meet resistance. If you must buy in, make your purchase at the bottom of the new price box which was established after the breakout.

While the Darvas method appears risky given its focus on only three or four high-growth stocks and buying into uptrends, the risk is controlled by buying into high-probability situations and stopping losses when you are wrong. The winners are huge, and one winner usually makes up for several losers. The key is timing your buys, cutting your losses, and focusing on the price behavior of the hottest stock in the market.

Chapter 7: My Darvas Stock Trades

I have deployed many strategies over the past ten years since my catastrophic loss of 50% of my investments after the Internet bubble burst. After the meltdown, my plan was actually buy and hold. I figured it was safe to start dollar-cost averaging back into my 401K since I did not have to worry about a market meltdown. Why? Because it had already happened: with most of the market down over 50% and tech stocks down some 80% or 90%, I figured I had a huge margin of safety, just as Warren Buffet likes to have before he invests his money. So as I positioned my 401K money into aggressive growth stock mutual funds, I began to contribute the maximum amount my company would match. With 5% of my income contributed, my company would allocate 4%; this was an 80% return on my money that I was not taxed on. In addition, this money would grow with no capital gains tax. All I had to do was buy at what I figured was a great price each month and wait.

This was the plan from 2000 until the recovery. I had gone from $60,000 in 2000 to dipping below $30,000 in 2003. The level of pain I experienced is hard to describe to anyone who has not gone through it. If you had a similar experience during the meltdown of 2008-2009, do not fret! If you have a long enough time horizon you can get it back. You just need the right strategy for the market conditions.

In 2002 the market was still dead and I kept buying into the market at lower and lower prices. My company started giving store managers 300 shares of stock options annually. My first 300-share option was at $28 and could be exercised to profit if the price of the stock increased over the option price. One hundred of the shares would be available after each year of employment. Within months of offering this benefit package, the stock promptly dove to $17 a share. Well, so much for that; I thought the stock was toast.

Within a year I was scrambling to find my options package as the stock exploded to over $48 a share and kept going alongside the rest of the market. With this amazing move upwards I decided to start deploying half of my 401K money to invest in the stock of my company (DEG). As the stock made new 52-week highs I felt secure in the earnings growth of the company and the interest of investors in the stock. I did not know it yet, but buying into strength and holding a stock as it breaks to higher all-time highs is the Darvas method.

By late 2004 I had returned to my original equity of $60,000 through buy-and-hold and dollar-cost averaging, along with (unknowingly at the time) using the Darvas method to load up on a hot stock with 50% of my available capital. I felt confident in an eventual recovery and I had been rewarded, but this was only the beginning. I was about to participate in a monster bull market.

By 2005 I had read Nicolas Darvas' book: "How I Made $2,000,000 in the Stock Market," and I realized that the market was beginning to trend higher. I began to watch my company's stock on my computer daily, even hourly sometimes. It began to pull away to an all-time high of $61 in September of 2004 and I was on board riding the highs. Reading the Darvas book a few months later gave me the confidence not to sell until it broke down out of its strong price boxes that were stacked one on top of the other. At the same time, my company was giving me and my wife 300 stock options a year. (My wife is also in management).

These options were not like the ones traded on the option exchange. These were simply 300 shares issued at the current market price that entitled you to profit in 100 of the shares each year for the next three years if the prevailing market price was more than the option price. As these options stacked on top of each other, we had the rights to almost 1,000 shares. In December 2004 the stock hit over $78 a share, then fell out of its box at $73, and I sold out of my 401K position before it plunged to $58. That is another Darvas method: Sell when the stock falls out of its current price box.

By the summer of 2006 it was back over $70 a share and breaking price boxes, going higher and higher. I was buying as it jumped to higher highs, hitting $83.70 by late September, pulling back, and then hitting 90 by March of 2007. It was quite enjoyable to see my account grow and grow day after day. I started playing the price boxes themselves, selling at the top of the box and buying on a $5 pullback, then selling again at the top of the box. This differed from the pure Darvas method, but it still used his box system. As Darvas explains, in his box system it is safe to buy at support so long as the stock does not fall below the established price box. In his third book, Darvas recommends shorting if a stock falls below the latest price box range. (He never shorted, as it went against his personality, but he validated the strategy).

The DEG stock finally hit an all-time high of $102.25 on July 23, 2007, as it pulled back to $99. Over the next few days I sold out of all my available options and took my 401K money back to mutual funds. That would be the all-time high, as the stock started to fall and did not fully stop until it hit a low of $43.68 on October 27, 2008. The beauty of the Darvas method is that I had sold out of my 401K and all my available options. I was not "waiting for the market to come back" or "buying a bargain" on the way down. Bottom fishers trying to buy in at a low price for an investment were wrong when they bought from $99 all the way down to $44.

There was a move from about $70 to almost $90 in early 2008 but it was choppy and volatile. This move was then followed by a dramatic plunge from $88 to $60.

Remember: Always buy into strength and sell into weakness. There is danger in volatility and in a market that moves up and down violently with little trend or reason. Trade in trending markets only and not in range bound markets if you want to trade like Darvas.

The pure Darvas method does not earn you profits at all-time highs; it gets you out as the support is lost and the downtrend begins. What it does do is give you the courage and guts to believe a stock will keep going higher until it is finished. I could have easily decided that the $61 all-time high was too high a price to pay and I would have missed out on an additional $41 move to $102.25. I also could have exercised my options too early and not waited for the big move. In bull markets, the hottest stocks have no resistance to higher and higher prices; in bear markets, most stocks have no solid low-price supports.

In a market downtrend stocks can fall to incredibly low levels, as was seen in March 2009. Readers must note that Darvas and I made these gains in bull markets with hot stocks. If you are unable to find stocks at all-time highs or at least 52-week highs, you are trying the right method in the wrong market; you are in a bear market. You would do better to short stocks that are at their all-time lows or 52-week lows. Darvas discusses this reverse system in his book: "You Can Still Make it in the Market." You simple reverse the system, selling short when a stock falls out of its box and covering if it rises back into its previous price box. In a winning short, you buy it back when it starts going up in price back through the previous price box.

With my winnings from my company-granted options I set up a margined broker account. I now had the freedom to play any stock. Where did I look for these Darvas stocks? The Investor's Business Daily 100 Top Stocks list is the best place to look for the strongest stocks in the market. You can either purchase access to these at the IBD website or buy or subscribe to the Monday edition of Investor's Business Daily. I began trading my brokerage account hitting and missing as the market grew choppier in late 2007. I was more or less breaking even buying on breakouts; I would win some and lose some.

Then I started watching Apple. On July 3, its all-time high was $122.09 while moving up box after box with higher highs. On that Friday I should have set a buy stop for $122.10 for the next day to capture the stock when it broke, but I thought I had time. This lack of discipline cost me. AAPL was trading at $128.80 at the open on Monday morning. I bought 100 shares at $130.84 Monday. July 5; it was trading at $132.75 at the close. The next day I bought another 100 shares at $132.25 and AAPL closed at $132.30. I waited. Over the next seven days it traded in a $129-$134 box, never pulling back anywhere near the $122.10 breakout. On July 12 I added an additional 100 shares at $133.37, as the earnings announcement grew near and excitement was at a high. Three days later I added my last 100 shares at $138.21. I now held 400 shares at an average price of $133.66.

Apple was a game changer for the music industry with the iPod and iTunes; this is the type of stock to look for in your Darvas trades – high volume and in the spotlight. AAPL ran out of gas and could not get above $145. I sold out 400 shares at an average price of $142.90 when the stock stalled before earnings. My net profit was $3,696. I was pleased with this, and it was my first really successful Darvas trade outside my 401K and company stock.

In late September of 2007, Research in Motion was on fire. Due to the huge Blackberry sales and profit expectations, the stock had been going up like a rocket for years. Blackberry changed its cell phones to smart phones and it was dominating its market. As the earnings announcement approached, RIMM broke its all-time high of $86.45 on September 13. I bought 100 shares at $87.10 and 100 shares at $88.06. Two days later I added 100 more at $87.27, then four days after that purchased 100 last shares at $92.28. As RIMM stayed nicely in a $93/$86 box (briefly at $85.42), I had no fear of it falling out of the box. The lows were brief and it went higher strongly.

Sometimes you have to give your trades room to work. With the first breakout coming on August 30 at $85, I felt confident that would be the best support to let RIMM breath. On September 26, two days before earnings were announced, RIMM shot up to $100.75, then fell to $97.95 before closing at $99. The next day it went to $100.98, then fell to $99.12. Earnings were drawing near and it appeared that it had run out of upward strength. This happens a lot in stocks, where round numbers act as resistance and people sell out when they see triple-digit stock prices for the first time. (This also happened in my DEG stock). I sold out of RIMM on September 27, 400 shares at $99.77 each for a profit of $4,440 on my second successful Darvas trade.

That same year I also traded Garman, the GPS maker, and Game Stop, the retail video game store. These trades were not successful like the AAPL and RIMM trades, and I gave back some of my profits. But I controlled my losses so they did not affect my account dramatically. The hottest stocks in the market were failing to make new all-time highs; this was a warning sign. As 2007 grew to a close, the market started to buzz with bad news about real estate, and interest rates were climbing; the Dow Jones Industrial Average and S&P 500 were topping out in early October 2007. Storm clouds were gathering, but I had one more Darvas trade to make. I went back to my beloved AAPL as it went to all-time highs a few days after my RIMM trade. On October 1 I bought AAPL at $154.63 as AAPL once again broke to new all-time highs. The next day I bought another 100 shares at $156.80, then four days later a final 100 shares at $158.02. I sold out on October 9, 300 shares for $168.35 for a $3,561 profit.

Through the fall of 2007 the market still failed to make higher highs, and it was becoming difficult to find any stocks making new highs. I lost on my attempted Darvas trades of AAPL for a third time and on Potash (POT). Both pulled back sharply before earnings and I was sold out for a loss. In late 2007 I had been entering the stock market on strength through mutual funds in my 401K and leaving on weakness when downtrends began. Due to the weakness on January 4, I went to cash in my 401K. Bad news seemed imminent on CNBC and fear was in the air. The technical price action was weak day after day. The market was far below its highs, along with all the previous hot stocks.

On January 4, CNBC was explaining the huge outflows of money from mutual funds and stocks into safer havens. This was the day I decided to vote along with the herd and cash in all my accounts. This proved to be the most profitable decision of my investing/trading career. Had I stayed in the markets or attempted to bottom fish back in my accounts, I would have likely melted down by over 50%. I did not return to stocks until March 2009, when once again I felt I had a margin of safety and would start dollar-cost averaging. I started moving my capital back into mutual funds in 25% increments. I was quickly scared out and lost the opportunity to catch the bottom. I was a Darvas investor by then and just could not bring myself to go into a bear market at any low. I did not reenter in any aggressive way with my 401K until the Dow was at 9500. I found no valid Darvas trades or safe investments in 2008 and 2009, and so I day traded for most of the time to reduce overnight risk.

I believe my success lies in the fact that I walked away with over $250,000 from my 401K, exercising my options and safely trading my brokerage account. From 2003 to 2007 I returned an average of over 20% in my 401K account; in 2008-2010 I earned returns of 3% to 4% in interest on my accounts with no draw-down in equity. So please, please, never let anyone tell you that it is impossible to time the market. There is a business cycle and stocks go up and down. There are recessions and depressions when stocks are annihilated. Educate yourself: buy in uptrends and sell in downtrends. If an Internet bubble pops, if terrorists attack the U.S., or if the real estate market collapses, for goodness' sake – go to cash!

Chapter 8: Winning the Game: So you want to trade like Nicolas Darvas?

If you want to trade like Nicolas Darvas, you must be willing to follow his rules and principles. One of the keys to his success was his ability to follow his rules and not his ego.

Discipline is the key to a trader's success, and a trading system is only as good as the trader who follows it. Most disciplined traders make money because they have the ability to follow a system that gives them an advantage over the market. Undisciplined traders usually lose most of their capital by taking too many large risks. Even if you win for a while, if you take large risks, one bad trade could ruin you if you do not cut your losses when your system confirms you are wrong. So if you want to trade like Nicolas Darvas you must follow his system, be disciplined, and avoid making up your own rules if you are forced to take a loss.

Darvas had the nerve to buy a stock as it broke to new highs. This is counter to most people's instincts who want to buy low and sell high. The truth is that during a bull market, a stock that is rocketing up because it is being acquired by mutual funds, hedge funds, or insiders may not give you a second chance to buy it back at a lower price until after the uptrend is over and it begins to be sold off – whether because of a change in the fundamental earnings expectations of the company or due to a technical top and subsequent price collapse. But the key is to buy it the moment it breaks out; do not chase it if you miss this breakout. That is why it is important to set buy stops that make that decision for you.

In his books, Darvas gives examples where he added to a position after a breakout while the stock was still in the box it broke into. If a stock is in a $95/$100 box, then breaks

$100.01 and rallies all the way to $105, it is safe to add to your initial position of $100.01 at $101 and $102, as long as the stock does not fall back under $100. In this example you still need to set your stop loss at $100 because that is a sell signal, since the stock falls back into a lower box. The key is that Darvas was a trend trader who bought into strength the moment a stock overcame all of the willing sellers at an old price and who bought at the pivotal moment when buyers were willing to buy at a higher price.

Nicolas Darvas removed his ego from investing by trading when the market was closed. He freed himself from having to make decisions under the pressure of a live market and moving prices. He examined the market prices and volume through Barron's each week when the market was closed. His stock broker also sent him daily quotes so he knew when he wanted to set a buy stop for a stock that was ready to break out to a new price box or move up a trailing stop after one of his holdings went to a new high in a new box. Darvas did not do well when he attempted to trade live during market hours or at brokerage houses with other traders, where he was swayed by their emotions to buy too late out of greed and sell too soon out of fear.

You have a huge advantage over the market when you make your decisions when you are completely rational and when the market is closed. In essence, your automatic orders are making the decisions for you. You can be successful in the market when your system is dictating your trades and not your own opinions. Darvas was a rule-based trader who used a system. It is very difficult for a person to outperform the market consistently, but there are many simple systems that outperform the market and are profitable. The Darvas system is one that has been proven over time. His system was one of the inspirations for William O'Neal, the founder of Investor's Business Daily and the CAN SLIM system.

Mr. O'Neal ran many historical tests on the greatest winning stocks of all time, and they were Darvas-type stocks. The Darvas system puts you into stocks that can double from $50 a share to $100 a share as they break to new highs and keep you in until the run is over.

Nicolas Darvas was a techno-fundamentalist and liked his stocks to be in new and exciting industry groups. He preferred the stock of companies that created huge earnings expectations for the future and that created excitement in the possibilities of unlimited growth. He also liked to put his money on the best company in that group, so long as the technical price action was breaking into a new all-time high on increasing volume. This was not always the case. If a stock started running up on heavy volume and breaking new price boxes, then Darvas had no problem joining other buyers even if he did not know why it was rocketing upwards. He let the price and volume of a stock tell its story. He did not attempt to "predict the market"; he did what the market told him to do. Stocks that were increasing to new highs on increased volume told him to buy. A stock sputtering and falling into an old price box told him to sell because the markets had lost interest in that stock.

Darvas tried not have opinions regarding a stock or the market. He designed his system to profit from the way the market worked rather than from his opinion of how it worked. He was successful: Through his system he earned over $2 million in profits in 18 months, and his system automatically sold him out to lock in profits before the raging bear market took hold after he had made his fortune. Some of the stocks he held during his huge winning streak went down 50%, 60%, 70% or more after he sold them. His system further protected him since it would not allow him to buy anything when no new highs in price were being made.

I took the Darvas system to heart and it told me to go to cash on January 4, 2008, which like Darvas enabled me to keep my bull market profits and saved me the mental anguish of the next two years when the Dow Jones Industrial Average sunk from its high of 14,164 on October 9, 2007, to an incredible low of 6,440 on March 9, 2009.

You must be aggressive in bull markets and cash in in bear markets. You have to be anxious to buy hot stocks as they break to all-time highs, and you do this by setting buy stops. You have to stop your losses with automatic stop losses when you are wrong. You have to be able to let your winners run until they stop running higher. You have to search for Darvas-type stocks in Investor's Business Daily, on the Internet via stock screeners, or you might hear about them on the news. When you find a product that will change an industry, a person's life, or the world, you may have found a Darvas stock.

Chapter 9: Rules

1. Identify stocks trading very close to their 52-week highs. (In Darvas' third book he changes from all-time highs to 52-week highs due to the severity of the bear market of his time. This can also apply to our time).

2. Identify stocks that are at least double their 52-week low from their current 52-week high.

3. Back check to ensure that the current 52-week high is also the stock's all-time high. (Be sure that you take into consideration stock splits when checking for the all-time high).

4. Look at charts or price histories to identify the price box they are in. If the 52-week high was $95 but in the last two weeks the stock traded as low as $90, then the price box would be $90/$95.

5. The stock needs to be trading on increasing volume over its past average volume. If the average volume was 250,000 shares over the last month when it traded at $90 to $95, then suddenly jumps to over a million shares as it breaks through $95, then you have a Darvas stock. If it breaks through that new high on lower than average volume – this is a danger sign and not a Darvas stock.

6. In the above example, you would purchase the stock at a breakout above $95. If you were waiting to buy at the breakout from the $90/$95 box, you would set a buy stop at $95.01. If the stock broke out above your buy stop then you would set a stop loss at the point of the breakout; your stop would be placed at $94.99. If your stock is a Darvas stock then it should not retrace into the old box; it should establish itself in a new box over the next few days such as at a high of $103 and a low of $97.

A box can be identified by three days of resisting a new high or three days of finding support at a new low. You may be stopped out several times in trades before you get the one trade where support holds and a new uptrend begins. Do not get discouraged. Your stop loss is your insurance against large losses. Darvas was stopped out many times before he got hold of the monster stocks that made him a fortune.

In Darvas' second book he recommends that a stock price must exceed the top of its box for three consecutive days before buying. In his third book he recommends buying after the retracement on the second breakout. This has caused his readers much confusion however this is simply Darvas' attempt to adjust his system as he continues to invest and learn. I have found his original system of buying at initial breakouts to be the most profitable. In raging bull markets you seldom get a second chance when monster stocks break loose at a high before earnings.

7. If the stock performs correctly you will reset and trail your loss behind it. If a stock then enters a $104-$109 box your stop loss will be below the bottom of the last box at $102.99.

8. Darvas was very aggressive and would make use of all of his available capital and margin when he took positions. The key to his risk management was that he was very disciplined and always made physical stop losses that acted as a trigger so that he could control his losses. Today, there is a danger that news will break when the market is closed and cause your stock to gap down and miss your stop the next morning. In this case, your stop loss should be triggered at the open the following day. While this will result in more losses than planned, on the upside, good news 'after hours' about your stock's company could cause your stock to gap up into a new box.

If you are going to trade like Nicolas Darvas, it is crucial that you follow his system and never override his stop loss policy. It is your insurance policy to prevent your ruin should something go terribly wrong and a trend in the stock that you own reverses violently.

9. In his third book Darvas recommends a maximum stop loss of 10% in any stock purchased, regardless of the price box range. He also recommends not giving back more than 20% in profits when you are in a winning position. This advice is necessary since the Darvas system does not allow for judgment.

If you decide to trade a volatile stock, you may have to set a stop at the bottom of its current box to allow it room to work. I would strongly advise against investing in any stock for which you cannot set the stop close to the breakout point. Like Darvas, at times you may also decide to buy a stock when it is close to the bottom of its box and sell it at the top for a nice swing trade. Swing trading will make you money most of the time, but the Darvas method in a rising market can make you rich. When real money is at stake people hate to lock in a loss, preferring to hope that the stock will rebound. Do not make this mistake: Cut your losses.

10. The Darvas rules are principles that can be used in all markets and in all timeframes.

- Set buy stops that will automatically buy at breakouts to new highs
  - Set stops to limit losses
  - Trail stops to lock in profits
  - Buy only the hottest stocks in major uptrends
  - Buy into strength; sell into weakness
  - Follow your rules not your ego
  - Remove fear and greed from your market actions
  - Only invest when your system gives a buy signal
  - Stay away from opinions; follow market action

Conclusion

I wrote this book to let readers know that you can make money in the stock market. Your 401K is a vehicle to wealth creation. It is a good idea to buy stocks as they make all-time highs for the first time and to stay away from stocks making new lows. If you want to trade the Darvas method, please wait until the next bull market. Pick the stocks that will change the world. Watch and study the personality of a stock's movement. Be aggressive and buy when it goes higher; be afraid when it fails to make new highs and goes lower through the current price box.

401K Investors: If the Darvas method is too scary for your sensibilities, then instead of buy and holding, at least use moving averages to identify trends. If you simply sell when the S&P dips below its 200-day moving average and buy as it goes above its 200-day moving average, you can double your investing performance over the long term. This also takes you out of bear markets early on and puts you back in bull markets at an early stage.

Never let anyone tell you that it is impossible to time the market. I have it for a decade, Nicolas Darvas did it, professionals do it every year, and so can you!

Recommended Reading

How I made $2,000,000 in the Stock Market

By: Nicolas Darvas

Wall Street: The Other Las Vegas

By: Nicolas Darvas

You Can Still Make it in the Market

By: Nicolas Darvas

An American Hedge Fund

By: Timothy Sykes

Trend Following

By: Michael Covel

CPSIA information can be obtained at www.ICGtesting.com
Printed in the USA
LVOW08s0308210815

450918LV00001B/168/P